MY
GROWTH
MINDSET
JOURNAL

MY GROWTH MINDSET JOURNAL

A TEACHER'S WORKBOOK TO
**REFLECT ON YOUR PRACTICE, CULTIVATE YOUR MINDSET,
SPARK NEW IDEAS** AND **INSPIRE STUDENTS**

ANNIE BROCK AND HEATHER HUNDLEY

Ulysses Press

Published in the United States by:
ULYSSES PRESS
P.O. Box 3440
Berkeley, CA 94703
www.ulyssespress.com

ISBN: 978-1-61243-836-8
Library of Congress Control Number: 2018944075

Printed in the United States by Bang Printing
10 9 8 7 6 5 4 3 2 1

Acquisitions editor: Casie Vogel
Managing editor: Claire Chun
Editor: Shayna Keyles
Proofreader: Renee Rutledge
Front cover design: Rebecca Lown
Interior design and layout: what!design @ whatweb.com

Distributed by Publishers Group West

INTRODUCTION

"Test scores and measures of achievement tell you where a student is, but they don't tell you where a student could end up."
—Carol Dweck

Hello, fellow educators! We are so happy you have joined us on this growth-mindset journey. *The Growth Mindset Journal* is designed to get you thinking and writing about your mindset at school. Make no mistake: Honest self-reflection is not an easy undertaking. It is challenging work that forces us to peel back the layers of our everyday experiences and confront our habits, values, and beliefs with an open mind and an open heart. As teachers, we experience so many daily decisions and interactions that it's easy to get caught up in the minutiae of the job, but when we take the time to look inward with a critical eye, we have the opportunity to see the bigger picture.

In her book, *Mindset*, Carol Dweck tells us, "Becoming is better than being." This journal is to help you *become*. When we operate in the fixed mindset, we saddle ourselves with false limitations. We trick ourselves out of going for what we truly want by convincing ourselves we are incapable, less than, or not destined for greatness. When we operate in the growth mindset, we have a fundamental belief in our

"There are no secrets to success. It is the result of preparation, hard work, and learning from failure."
—Colin Powell

ability to change, grow, and achieve. We want you to embrace the growth mindset as a perpetual state of *becoming*. If you allow yourself, you can always learn, grow, and take the path to a deeper understanding. The journey down that path begins with the first step of self-discovery.

There is no right way to interact with this journal. You might start from the beginning and work your way through, close your eyes and open to a random page each day, or pick it up once every few weeks when the mood to write strikes you. It's not important how you engage in self-reflection; it's only important that you do. There are a variety of topics, idea starters, question-and-response scenarios, doodle tasks, and journal prompts in these pages. We've also included pages at the end of the journal that simply say "My day at school…," because sometimes you have something you need to get out that doesn't follow a prompt or guideline, and that's okay, too.

Think of this journal as a favor you do for yourself each day. Sit in a quiet place with a favorite drink—some days might call for coffee, others for wine—and reflect on your day. Put aside the stress, chaos, and noise, and take a moment to reflect on experiences you didn't have time to ponder when they occurred. Be kind to yourself at your worst and grateful at your best. The more you write and reflect, the more you will see patterns emerge. You will see people who consistently lift you up. You will relish in routines you failed to notice before. You will make connections between your fixed mindset and what triggers it. You will come to a greater understanding about the habits, experiences, and people who help you be your favorite version of yourself.

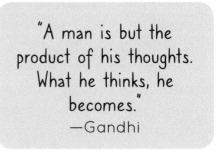

"A man is but the product of his thoughts. What he thinks, he becomes."
—Gandhi

The growth mindset, in its purest form, allows us to view challenges and obstacles not simply as things to get through, but things to learn from. Give yourself the gift of mindfulness; allow your observations to flourish into a web of new ideas. When we have a true understanding of our thoughts, words, and actions, they can propel us to heights previously unimagined. Use these pages to write your story; give yourself the gift of *becoming*.

Henry Ford said, "Whether you think you can or can't, you're right." Describe what this quote means to you.

....

....

....

....

....

....

....

....

....

....

....

....

Let's get to know each other. Draw a self-portrait of you on a typical school day.

Explain why you chose certain details for your portrait. Messy bun? Pencil behind your ear? Cheeky smile? Ketchup stain on your shirt? Reflect on your self-portrait as an expression of how you see yourself at school.

List three ways you can positively greet students in the morning.

1.
....
....
....
....

2.
....
....
....
....

3.
....
....
....
....

"All progress takes place outside the comfort zone."
—Michael John Bobak

A "fixed mindset" is the belief that we're born with a fixed amount of intelligence, skills, and abilities, and we cannot do much to meaningfully change that. Write your definition of fixed mindset and how you see it at play in the world around you.

....

....

....

....

....

....

Everyone has a growth mindset and a fixed mindset. The mindset with which you approach any given situation can perpetuate your thoughts and actions and influence the outcome.

Describe a time your growth mindset inspired thoughts and actions, leading to a positive outcome.

Describe a time your fixed mindset inspired thoughts and actions, leading to a negative outcome.

Think of a person or character that models growth-mindset behaviors. Write about them.

Positive relationships are fundamental drivers of growth mindsets in the classroom. Your attitudes toward students and your belief in their ability to succeed propel them to take risks, ask questions, and be vulnerable learners. Describe how you cultivate positive relationships among your students. What could you do better?

"Anyone who stops learning is old, whether at twenty or eighty.
Anyone who keeps learning stays young."
—Henry Ford

List five new things you want to learn or do.

1.

2.

3.

4.

5.

Draw your brain in the growth-mindset zone. What imagery, words, and phrases frequent your thoughts when you're overcoming a challenging situation, in the midst of a struggle, or rising after a fall?

How do you think the following people or groups of people perceive your mindset? Why?

1. Students
....

....

....

2. Supervisors
....

....

....

3. Family
....

....

....

4. Coworkers
....

....

....

5. Friends
....

....

....

"A teacher affects eternity; he can never tell where his influence stops."
—Henry Adams

"Teaching is a practice, not a perfection." What does this saying mean to you?

....

....

....

....

....

....

....

....

....

....

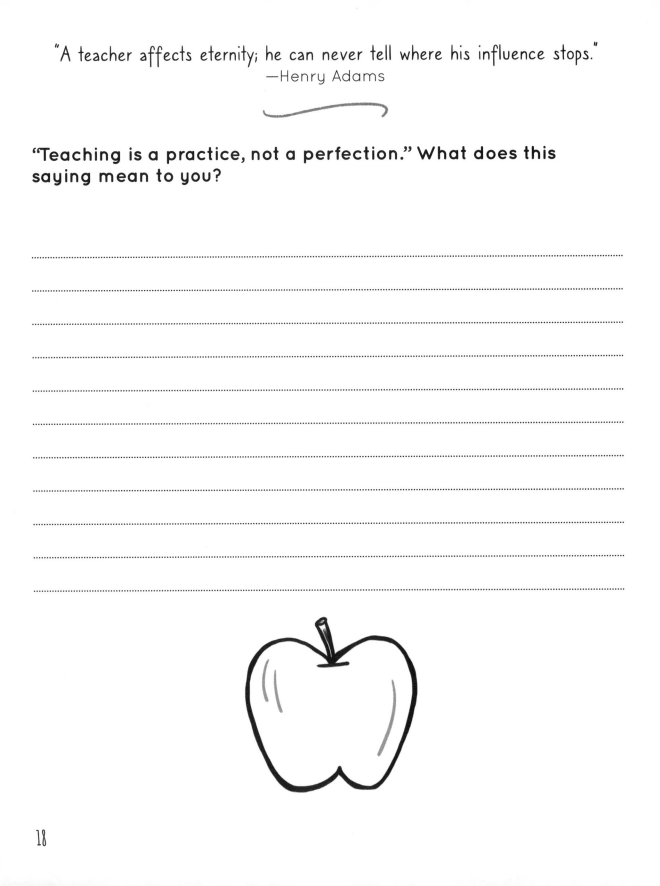

What is something you need to let go of? Write it inside the balloon and symbolically release it.

At school, we often treat "struggle" like a four-letter word, but attempting to insulate students against struggling with schoolwork is actually counterproductive. Giving students the opportunity to wrestle with difficult challenges and tasks, and encouraging them to see it through to the end, actually helps develop growth mindsets.

Describe what advice you would give to students in the midst of struggle to help them persist in the face of a challenge.

Write about how growth mindset has changed the way you teach.

....

....

....

....

....

....

....

....

....

....

In terms of learning and growth, that three-letter word can be a powerful motivator. Built into that little word is hope and potential; it represents a future time when success will come, if only we can persist through the now. Some schools even offer a grade of "not yet" instead of Ds and Fs. Write about how harnessing the power of "yet" might foster growth mindsets among your students.

....

....

....

....

....

....

....

....

....

YET

"Strength and growth come only through continuous effort and struggle."
—Napoleon Hill

Write down three things that you're good at:

1.
....

....

2.
....

....

3.
....

....

Now, choose one item from your list and explain the effort you have put forth to become good at it.

....

....

....

....

Write about the last thing you read or heard that inspired you.

....

....

....

....

....

....

....

....

....

....

Picture your most difficult student. Write down three things you can do tomorrow to build your relationship with him or her.

1. ....

....

....

....

....

2. ....

....

....

....

....

3. ....

....

....

....

....

"There are better starters than me but I'm a strong finisher."
—Usain Bolt

Jot down a growth mindset message you can review when you feel rooted in your fixed mindset.

Normalizing mistakes is a key value of a growth-mindset classroom. We want students to view mistakes as important tools for learning. In math class, this makes sense, but what about when it comes to behavior? Giving students an opportunity to reflect on a behavioral mistake and devise a strategy for changing the behavior can be a powerful force for cultivating growth in the classroom.

Think about your behavior management plan. How does it foster growth mindset?

....

....

....

....

....

....

"Success seems to be connected with action. Successful people keep moving. They make mistakes, but they don't quit."
—Conrad Hilton

What teaching mistake do you need to forgive yourself for? Do it here.

....

....

....

....

....

....

....

....

....

"Love me when I least deserve it, because that's when I really need it."
—Swedish Proverb

Can you recall a time when you needed love, but you received judgment, disrespect, or punitive consequences? How could unconditional positive regard have been used to demonstrate care and respect and provide an opportunity to grow from the mistake?

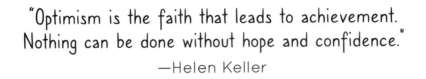

*"Optimism is the faith that leads to achievement.
Nothing can be done without hope and confidence."*
—Helen Keller

Think back about a teacher whose belief in your ability to succeed was transformational. Write about that teacher.

In what ways do you consider yourself a learner?

Many schools and classrooms are driven by competition, but this type of environment can breed an "every man for himself" attitude among students, which fosters fixed mindsets. Promoting positive interdependence in your classroom means creating an environment in which all members are working toward common goals and playing a valuable role in achieving those goals. Write about how you promote interdependence in your classroom.

....

....

....

....

....

....

> *"Every strike brings me closer to the next home run."*
> —Babe Ruth

What is a challenge you are currently facing? Write about a strategy you can use to overcome the challenge.

"Growth mindset" is the belief that intelligence and other qualities, abilities, and talents can be developed with effort, learning, and dedication over time. Write your definition of growth mindset and how you see it at play in the world around you.

....

....

....

....

....

....

....

....

List three ways you can positively greet colleagues in the morning.

1. ....

....

....

2. ....

....

....

3. ....

....

....

Respond to this quote:

"Courage is not the absence of fear, but rather the judgment that
something else is more important than fear."
—Ambrose Redmoon

....

....

....

....

....

....

....

....

....

....

"Would you like me to give you a formula for success? It's quite simple, really. Double your rate of failure."
—Thomas Watson

An important aspect of growth mindset is embracing failure as an opportunity to learn. What practices do you have in place in your classroom that facilitate students' ability to grow from mistakes and failures?

Describe a time when you experienced productive struggle.

....

....

....

....

....

....

....

....

....

....

What did you do today that showcased your growth mindset?

....

....

....

....

....

....

....

....

....

....

TODAY!

14

"Happiness is not something ready-made. It comes from your own actions."
—The XIV Dalai Lama

Draw an image that represents a growth mindset.

Think of a time that you failed at something. Write a thank you note to your failure telling it how it helped you grow.

Modeling your growth mindset is key to helping your students develop their own. Think about a time when you made a mistake or failed at something and grew from the experience. Write it down here. (Bonus! Share your response with your students. How do they react?)

"One person can make a difference, and everyone should try."
—John F. Kennedy

Name three things you can do tomorrow to make a difference in the lives of others.

1.

2.

3.

Think about a person (or people) in your life that has a growth mindset. Write down the name of the person and, specifically, how they have demonstrated a growth mindset.

....

....

....

....

....

....

....

....

....

"Leaders are made, they are not born. They are made by hard effort, which is the price which all of us must pay to achieve any goal that is worthwhile."
—Vince Lombardi

Describe what a successful teacher looks like. Write about how you meet your description and how you fall short of it.

....

....

....

....

....

....

....

....

What frustrates you at school? Write one thing you can do tomorrow to work toward making it better.

Make a list of your fixed-mindset triggers.

*"Success is the ability to go from one failure to another
with no loss of enthusiasm."*
—Anonymous

How do you encourage enthusiasm for learning and growth in your classroom?

....

....

....

....

....

....

....

....

Think about your classroom expectations. How do your rules promote a growth-oriented environment?

"Two roads diverged in a wood, and I, I took the one less traveled by, and that has made all the difference."
—Robert Frost

Draw an image that represents a fixed mindset.

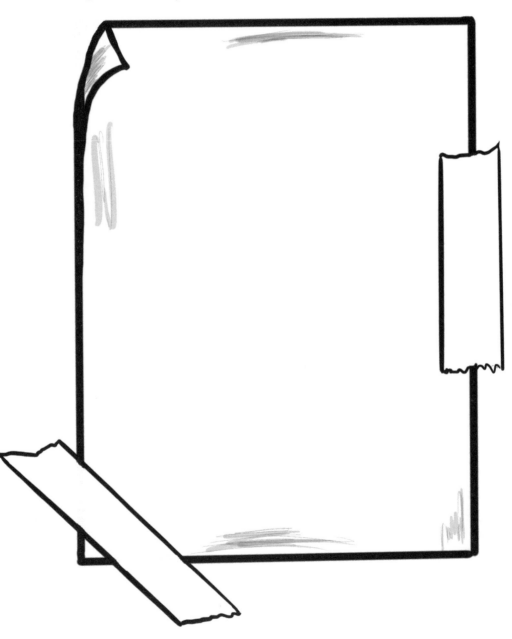

Consider your grading practices for a moment. How do grades promote a growth mindset in your class? If they don't, how could you change your practices so they do?

....

....

....

....

....

....

....

....

....

Think of a time when one of your students was able to rise above failure or fear and achieve a goal. How did it make you feel? If you could write a note to this student, what would it say?

....

....

....

....

....

....

....

....

....

Describe the best experience you have ever had as a learner.

....
....
....
....
....
....
....
....
....
....

"The real test is not whether you avoid this failure, because you won't. It's whether you let it harden or shame you into inaction, or whether you learn from it; whether you choose to persevere."
—Barack Obama

Think about a time you failed at something you really wanted to achieve. Describe how you responded to the failure with a fixed or growth mindset.

"You can't use up creativity. The more you use, the more you have."
—Maya Angelou

Employers agree that one of the most desirable traits in a potential employee is the ability to solve problems. In order to be a problem solver, one must be a creative thinker, go back to the drawing board when necessary, and look at problems from new and interesting angles. Problem-solving and growth mindset go hand in hand. The ability to persist, iterate, and try, try again is what growth mindset is all about!

Describe how you promote and encourage problem-solving in your classroom.

Write about why the journey of learning is more important than the destination.

....

....

....

....

....

....

....

....

....

Teaching is an emotionally, physically, and mentally exhausting job. How do you practice self-care?

If you had to choose a motto for life, what would it be and why?

Philanthropist John Lubbock said, "What we see depends mainly on what we look for." There is, perhaps, no place this quote rings more true than in the classroom. List the top five things that you look for in the classroom. (Hint: Think about what you consistently praise, reward, and correct if you're unsure.) How does what you look for in students influence student behavior?

1. ....

2. ....

3. ....

4. ....

5. ....

Think about a fixed-mindset message you tell yourself, and write it down. (For example: I'm not artistic, I'm not a math person, etc.) How did you come to this belief, and how does it limit you?

_____

_____

_____

_____

_____

_____

_____

_____

_____

_____

_____

_____

_____

_____

What would a growth-oriented report card look like?

REPORT CARD

"Show me someone who has done something worthwhile, and I'll show you someone who has overcome adversity."
—Lou Holtz

In the growth mindset, we are not threatened by the success of others; rather, we are inspired by it. Think of someone who is achieving success in a way that you would like to. How can you learn from that person?

....

....

....

....

....

....

....

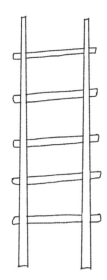

List five things that you truly enjoy about being an educator.

1. ....

....

2. ....

....

3. ....

....

4. ....

....

5. ....

....

Write about how you can use growth mindset to introduce a new concept or learning challenge.

....

....

....

....

....

....

....

....

....

....

"The greatest glory in living lies not in never falling,
but in rising every time we fall."
—Oliver Goldsmith

Success is less about perfection than it is about persistence. A pernicious myth in our culture is that success comes easy to those who are destined for it. But most successful people will tell you that this is not the case. Rather, the path to success is littered with mistakes, failures, setbacks, and moments of wanting to throw in the towel.

Think about someone who is successful in a certain field. Do a little research to find out the hard work and failures that contributed to their success. Record your findings below.

Write down three things that you're bad at, but would like to be better at:

1. ....
....
....
....
....

2. ....
....
....
....
....

3. ....
....
....
....
....

Write about a time you witnessed a student move from a fixed mindset to a growth mindset.

....

....

....

....

....

....

....

....

....

....

....

....

....

....

....

....

> "When a flower doesn't bloom, you fix the environment in which it grows, not the flower."
> —Alexander den Heijer

In a safe and nurturing learning environment, students feel free to take educational risks. How do you ensure your classroom or learning environment is safe and nurturing? How could you improve it? List the ways.

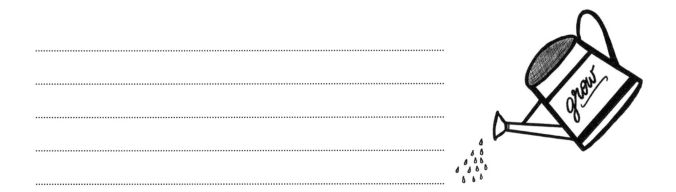

....

....

....

....

....

Now, choose one item from your list and specifically explain how you could potentially improve in that area. (And, go ahead, give it a try this week!)

....

....

....

....

....

....

Historian Thomas Fuller said, "All things are difficult before they are easy." Write about what this means to you.

....

....

....

....

....

....

....

....

....

Draw your brain in the fixed-mindset zone. What imagery, words, and phrases frequent your thoughts when you're avoiding a problem, feeling insecure, or making excuses after a failure?

"The only limit to our realization of tomorrow will be our doubts of today."
—Franklin D. Roosevelt

Imagine your classroom, or take a look around if you're sitting in it. Describe how it serves to empower learners.

....

....

....

....

....

....

....

....

Goal setting can promote growth mindset because it charts a course for achieving a goal and breaks the required work into manageable steps. When students accomplish a goal they have set, they can see the path from hard work to achievement.

Write about how you use (or could use) goal setting in your classroom.

....

....

....

....

....

....

....

Write your response to a parent who tells you people in their family "just aren't [insert subject here**] kind of people."**

In her book, *Mindset*, Carol Dweck writes, "Becoming is better than being." Write about what this means to you.

....

....

....

....

....

....

....

....

....

Write about how you set expectations for your students.

Artist Salvador Dali once said, "Have no fear of perfection. You'll never reach it." Write about a time being a perfectionist backfired on you.

....

....

....

....

....

....

....

....

Describe the best experience you have ever had as a teacher.

....

....

....

....

....

....

....

....

....

....

WORLD'S BEST TEACHER

"You miss 100 percent of the shots you don't take."
—Wayne Gretzky

On a scale of 1 to 10, how was your growth mindset today? Write about it.

Write an apology to someone who was negatively affected by your fixed mindset.

....

....

....

....

....

....

....

....

....

....

....

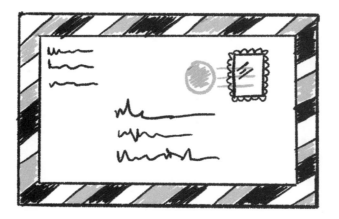

Write down the names of some specific students who have been challenging to teach. Describe how you have seen each of those students grow or how they have a unique opportunity for growth in the right conditions.

....

....

....

....

....

....

....

....

"You just can't beat the person who never gives up."
—Babe Ruth

>————————<

What is something in your life that you gave up on? Why did you quit?

If you've ever faced a difficult problem or challenge, tussled around with it for a while, and then—click—figured it out, you've experienced what we in the learning biz like to call the "light bulb moment." In his book, *Helping Children Succeed*, Paul Tough writes, "When students get a chance to experience those moments, no one has to persuade them, in an abstract or theoretical way, of the principles of a growth mindset. They intuitively believe that their brains grow through effort and struggle, and they believe it for the best possible reason: because they can feel it happening."

Write about a time when you felt learning happening in your life.

....

....

....

....

....

....

....

....

....

....

Normalizing mistakes in your classroom is a powerful way to help students feel safety and freedom to take educational risks. From a student perspective, what does making a mistake look and feel like in your classroom?

....

....

....

....

....

....

....

....

....

....

....

....

....

....

"You are never too old to set another goal or to dream a new dream."
—Les Brown

Write about how self-reflection plays a critical role in developing growth mindset.

....

....

....

....

....

....

....

....

Pretend a student is working on a particularly challenging math assignment. He throws up his hands and declares, "I'm just not a math person!" Write five ways you could respond to him to encourage his growth mindset.

1.

2.

3.

4.

5.

"Freedom is not worth having if it does not connote freedom to err."
—Gandhi

Write about how you demonstrate to your students that you are a learner, too.

....

....

....

....

....

....

....

....

Dr. Jerome Bruner, said, "You more likely act yourself into feeling than feel yourself into action." Sometimes we have to act in ways that are incongruous to our feelings at school.

Talk about a time you had to fake it, and describe how intentionally acting in that manner ultimately changed your way of thinking.

....

....

....

....

....

....

....

....

....

....

....

....

....

"Dreams don't work unless you do."
—John C. Maxwell

Write about one thing you can do tomorrow to promote growth mindsets in your classroom.

There's a saying, "Don't let perfect be the enemy of good." Think of a time a result fell short of your hopes and expectations. Did you let the absence of a perfect outcome prevent you from recognizing some evidence of growth or improvement? Describe that experience.

....

....

....

....

....

....

....

....

Write about the difference between the desire to learn and the desire to succeed.

....

....

....

....

....

....

....

....

....

....

....

....

....

....

....

....

....

Humorist David Sedaris said, "I haven't got the slightest idea how to change people, but still I keep a long list of prospective candidates just in case I should ever figure it out." In a perfect world, we'd be able to convince people to change, but that's not the reality. We cannot force students to have a growth mindset, but we can create conditions in which their growth mindsets can flourish.

Name five things that you do or can do to foster growth mindsets among students.

1. ....

....

2. ....

....

3. ....

....

4. ....

....

5. ....

....

Imagine a student has set a goal and failed to accomplish it. What do you do next?

"Tell me and I forget. Teach me and I remember. Involve me and I learn."
—Benjamin Franklin

When you experience failure, who do you turn to for encouragement? Write about how that person helps you cope with failure.

....

....

....

....

....

....

....

....

Write three things you love about your school.

1. ....

....

....

2. ....

....

....

3. ....

....

....

Carol Dweck writes in *Mindset*, "If parents want to give their children a gift, the best thing they can do is teach their children to love challenges, be intrigued by mistakes, enjoy effort, and keep on learning." How can you teach parents to extend growth-mindset practices from the school to the home?

When success doesn't come right away, how can you help students understand the value of growth over time?

....

....

....

....

....

....

....

....

....

....

....

Think about a time that you learned something new, such as how to back a car out of the driveway, how to roller skate, or how to ride a bicycle. What were the steps involved in the learning? Did you have failures along the way?

You're faced with a fixed-mindset trigger. Write about your go-to strategies for avoiding falling into a fixed-mindset trap.

"Make each day your masterpiece."
—John Wooden

Describe some characteristics of a student with a growth mindset.

Confucius said, "It does not matter how slowly you go, so long as you do not stop." Write about a time when you struggled to master something and your persistence paid off.

....

....

....

....

....

....

....

....

....

What challenged you today?

....

....

....

....

....

....

....

....

....

....

In the fixed mindset, challenges are often avoided to maintain the appearance of intelligence. Imagine a conversation between you and a student who is avoiding a challenge. What do you say to motivate and inspire that student to tackle learning challenges head on?

....

....

....

....

....

....

....

....

"If you hear a voice within you saying 'you are not a painter,' then by all means paint and that voice will be silenced."
—Vincent Van Gogh

A student paints a beautiful picture in art class. Instead of saying, "Wow! You're a gifted artist," what growth-oriented praise could you offer the student?

....

....

....

....

....

....

....

Think about your morning routine at school. Describe adjust-ments you could make to inspire growth mindsets at the beginning of the day.

....

....

....

....

....

....

....

....

....

....

....

....

Write about something you observed at school today that inspires you.

"There is nothing noble in being superior to your fellow man; true nobility is being superior to your former self."
—Ernest Hemingway

Think about your most challenging student. Write three things that you like about that student.

1. ....

....

....

2. ....

....

....

3. ....

....

....

Carol Dweck said, "A person's true potential is unknown and unknowable. It is impossible to foresee what can be accomplished with years of passion, toil, and training." Write about a time you felt limited by someone's belief about your potential. How did you overcome it?

"The most effective way to do it is to do it."
—Amelia Earhart

Describe the conditions in which you do your best learning.

Offering progress-focused, growth-oriented praise is an excellent strategy for fostering growth mindsets among your students. Write down three examples of growth-oriented praise that you might offer a student who has done well on an exam.

1. ....

....

....

2. ....

....

....

3. ....

....

....

How do you incorporate student voice and choice in your classroom?

"If you do what you've always done, you'll get what you've always gotten."
—Tony Robbins

No one is immune from falling into the fixed mindset. Everyone falls into fixed-mindset traps of avoiding challenges, feeling professional jealousies, or casting blame on another for their own shortcomings. Describe a time you fell into a fixed-mindset trap. Did you get yourself out? If so, how?

In the immediate aftermath of a student failure, how can you use that moment as an opportunity to promote growth?

Witnessing the success of others in a field or at a task we would like to find success in can often trigger a fixed mindset by evoking feelings of insecurity. Describe a time your fixed mindset has been triggered because another person succeeded.

Write about how you promote a culture of hard work and effort in your classroom.

"Kind words can be short and easy to speak,
but their echoes are truly endless."
—Mother Teresa

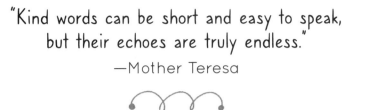

In the growth mindset, we are inspired by the success of others. In the fixed mindset, we are resentful of the success of others. Talk about a time you had a success and were met with resentment from someone instead of positivity.

....

....

....

....

....

....

....

Write three things you say to yourself to reframe your mindset from fixed to growth.

1.

2.

3.

"Never interrupt someone doing something you said couldn't be done."
—Amelia Earhart

Describe some characteristics of a student with a fixed mindset.

Write your name below with your non-dominant hand.

....

....

....

....

....

....

Now, describe how it felt to write your name with the wrong hand. Awkwardness, frustration, irritation—these are feelings often evoked when learning something new or doing something for the first time. How might you compare writing with your non-dominant hand to learning a difficult concept or skill?

....

....

....

....

....

....

Write about how certain grading and assessment practices can trigger fixed mindsets.

....

....

....

....

....

....

....

....

....

....

....

....

....

....

....

....

....

Perhaps one of the most powerful strategies for fostering growth mindset in your classroom is modeling growth mindset. Create a plan for how you can be more intentional in modeling your growth mindset for students.

"When everything seems to be going against you, remember that the airplane takes off against the wind, not with it."
—Henry Ford

Write about a time you had to embrace a big change. What role did your mindset play in accepting (or not accepting) the change?

....

....

....

....

....

....

....

....

....

....

....

....

....

....

Write a letter to your administrator about why growth mindset is an essential part of school culture.

....
....
....
....
....
....
....
....
....
....
....

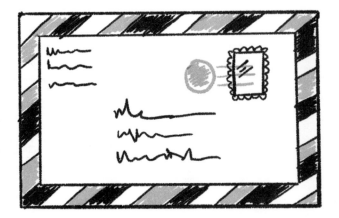

One strategy we suggest using to confront your fixed mindset is to give it a name. That way you can address it directly when you send it packing. What would you name your fixed mindset and why? (Hint: This is a great exercise to do with students. The names they create for their fixed mindsets will provide your daily comic relief!)

Think about a book, song, movie, anecdote, etc., that demonstrates the value of a growth mindset, and share it with your students. Facilitate a discussion on growth and fixed mindset. How did the students respond to what you shared?

"It is hard to fail, but it is worse never to have tried to succeed."
—Theodore Roosevelt

Think about something you've been struggling with at school. Write down three strategies you could try to overcome the problem.

1.
....
....
....

2.
....
....
....

3.
....
....

Educator Dr. Kevin Maxwell writes, "Our job is to teach the students we have. Not the ones we would like to have. Not the ones we used to have. Those we have right now. All of them." Think about this quote. Do you ever find yourself wishing for different students? Write down how you can better focus your energy and efforts on the students you have right now.

Write a letter to your fixed mindset.

How did you grow today?

"I've learned that people will forget what you said, people will forget what you did, but people will never forget how you made them feel."
—Maya Angelou

Write about a student that made a lasting impression on you. What qualities did this student have? What experiences did you share? Why do you think this student stands out in your memory?

What does YET mean to you?

"The only man who never makes a mistake
is the man who never does anything."
—Theodore Roosevelt

Write about a persistent memory of a time that you failed with
a student. Maybe you lost your cool. Maybe you were overly
harsh or unforgiving, or didn't show grace when it was needed
most. (We've all been there.) Describe the situation and write
about what you might have done differently.

Write about something new that you've tried this school year.

....

....

....

....

....

....

....

....

....

....

Think about a student in your class who has demonstrated growth recently, whether in learning, relationships, or behavior. Call that student's parent or caretaker and describe the positive growth, expressing your happiness in their progress— say nothing negative on this call. Write down the response of the parent or caretaker, and how you felt after making the call.

....

....

....

....

....

....

....

....

What's in your teaching comfort zone and what is just outside it?

We want our students to be successful, but often we fail to set them up for success. Describe how you make an effort to set students up for success. How could you do it better?

"The greatest mistake you can make in life is to be continually fearing you will make one."
—Elbert Hubbard

How was your fixed mindset triggered today?

"We're educators. We're born to make a difference."
—Rita Pierson

Teachers love a good "a-ha!" moment. Describe one of these moments when a student mastered a particularly sticky concept they'd been wrestling with for a while. How did it make you feel? What did you learn from it?

....

....

....

....

....

....

....

The main driver of the fixed mindset is fear: fear of failure, fear of embarrassment, fear of being found out as a fraud, fear of not achieving your dreams. Think about a fear that drives your fixed mindset and write a letter to your fear.

....

....

....

....

....

....

....

....

....

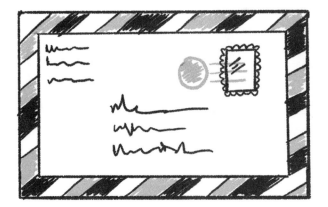

Write five things you could say to a student who has done well instead of "You're so smart!"

1. ....

....

2. ....

....

3. ....

....

4. ....

....

5. ....

....

Teaching has a ripple effect. Sometimes the seeds we plant now don't flourish in our students until years later. How does your role in the future of other people make you feel?

....

....

....

....

....

....

....

....

....

....

....

....

....

....

"We all need people who will give us feedback. That's how we improve."
—Bill Gates

How do you use effective feedback to promote growth mindsets among your students?

Which statement most reflects your current thoughts about growth-mindset messaging and the impact it can have on student learning? Write about it.

- I disagree that it can make an impact.

- I'm skeptical of the benefits of growth mindset.

- I really don't know yet.

- It is helpful in student learning.

- It is essential to student growth and learning.

"Every child deserves a champion; an adult who will never give up on them, who understands the power of connection and insists that they become the best they can possibly be."

—Rita Pierson

Meaningful praise and encouragement are essential tools in the growth-mindset educator's toolbox. How do you give growth-oriented praise and encouragement?

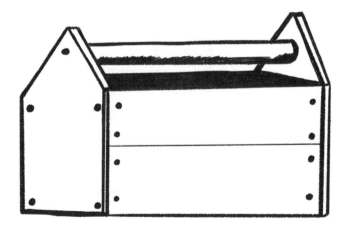

Write about how you could foster growth mindset in your whole-school community.

....
....
....
....
....
....
....
....
....
....

Metacognition is often defined as "thinking about thinking." In other words, taking time to reflect on the strategies you depend on as a learner is a critical process of growth. Write down your strategies for successful learning.

As a bonus activity, ask your students to make a list of how they learn best. What surprises you? How can you incorporate individual learning styles and strategies into your classroom?

Write about how you can bring a growth mindset to professional development.

"It's kind of fun to do the impossible."
—Walt Disney

How do you empower students to drive their own learning?

"I am not a product of my circumstances. I am a product of my decisions."
—Stephen Covey

List five things that you think you do well in teaching.

1.
....

....

2.
....

....

3.
....

....

4.
....

....

5.
....

....

Imagine you're having a conversation with a colleague in the work room. The colleague begins talking about a specific student in a negative way, including things like, "He just doesn't care," and "He'll never amount to anything." How do you use growth mindset attitude to respond to the colleague's fixed mindset about the student?

How is your feedback to students meaningful, relevant, and growth-oriented?

Write about a time you encountered a colleague with a fixed mindset.

Evidence shows us that success is achieved through effort, hard work, and perseverance, and not just raw talent. When a student effortlessly achieves top grades in your class, it may be because the work is not challenging enough. How do you ensure that every student in your class is being sufficiently challenged in a way that necessitates grit and hard work?

"Setting a goal is not the main thing. It is deciding how you will go about achieving it and staying with that plan."
—Tom Landry

List five things you believe you could improve in your teaching.

1.

2.

3.

4.

5.

Write about something new you learned this week.

"Failing forward" is learning from a failure in a way that propelled you toward greater understanding. Write about a time that you failed forward.

Passionate teachers have an opportunity to transform and inspire students to be curious, ask questions, and take on self-learning. How do you strive to be a multidimensional teacher that engages students in problem solving, wonder, and learning?

Write about a time a student triggered your fixed mindset.

Albert Einstein said, "It's not that I'm so smart, it's just that I stay with problems longer." What does this mean to you?

....

....

....

....

....

....

....

....

....

....

"Emotion is contagious."
—Malcolm Gladwell

Picture a student with whom you'd like to create a closer connection. Write five things you know about the student (likes, dislikes, interests, hobbies, qualities, habits, etc.) that you could use as a springboard for building a relationship.

1.
....

....

2.
....

....

3.
....

....

4.
....

....

5.
....

....

Write about a time a colleague or administrator triggered your fixed mindset.

Helping your students set and pursue measurable, achievable learning goals is critical in a growth-oriented classroom. Write about how goal setting can foster growth mindsets.

....

....

....

....

....

....

....

....

Write about a time you struggled to overcome a learning challenge. How did it make you feel?

....

....

....

....

....

....

....

....

....

....

....

....

....

....

....

....

"When it is obvious that the goals cannot be reached, don't adjust the goals, adjust the action steps."
—Chinese proverb

≪━━━━━≫

Write about the physical, social, and emotional responses that you observe when a student is struggling.

....

....

....

....

....

....

....

....

....

....

....

....

....

....

Think of a time you approached a situation with a fixed mind-set. Now, reimagine the situation as if you had approached it with a growth mindset. How might it have turned out differently?

People in the fixed mindset often blame others for their own shortcomings as a way to avoid accepting responsibility for failure. Write about a time you blamed another person for your failure or a time that someone blamed you for theirs.

....

....

....

....

....

....

....

....

....

....

....

....

....

....

....

How do you communicate growth mindset to parents? What could you do better or differently to help families foster growth mindsets at home?

....

....

....

....

....

....

....

....

"You must do the things you think you cannot do."
—Eleanor Roosevelt

Think about a time you had to rise above your fear. Write about it.

How do you intentionally create a learning environment in which it is okay for students to fail and make mistakes?

In *Mindset*, Carol Dweck writes, "It's not always the people who start out the smartest who end up the smartest." Write about an experience you've had as a teacher or learner that exemplifies Dr. Dweck's observation.

"Don't give up. Don't ever give up."
—Jimmy Valvano

Write about how you respond when a student gives up.

....

....

....

....

....

....

....

....

....

....

....

....

....

....

Write three things your administrator could do to promote growth mindset among teachers at your school.

1.
....
....
....
....
....

2.
....
....
....
....
....

3.
....
....
....
....
....

John Wayne once said, "Courage is being scared to death but saddling up anyway." Write about a time you saddled up anyway.

....

....

....

....

....

....

....

....

....

....

....

Describe an engaged student. What does engagement look like?

"The best competition I have is against myself—to become better."
—John Wooden

Write about a time you turned a disastrous lesson plan, teaching mistake, or another mishap at school into an opportunity to model growth mindset.

Dweck identified five areas in which the actions of people diverge depending on their mindset: challenges, obstacles, effort, criticism, and success of others. Where do you often see your fixed-mindset self-talk emerge?

Thomas Jefferson said, "I find that the harder I work, the more luck I seem to have." Write about what this means to you.

....

....

....

....

....

....

....

....

Think about an important conversation you recently experienced. What fixed- or growth-mindset messages were conveyed? Describe your mindset in the conversation.

What is the best mistake you have ever made? Why was it a mistake? What did you learn from it?

Businessman and philanthropist John Shedd said, "A ship in harbor is safe, but that is not what ships are build for." Write about what this quote means to you.

....

....

....

....

....

....

....

....

....

Write about a time this week when your fixed mindset overruled your growth mindset. Looking back, how or what could you have done to foster your growth-mindset message?

What would you say to your best friend who just experienced failure?

"Strength does not come from physical capacity. It comes from an indomitable will."
—Gandhi

What does perseverance look like, sound like, and feel like?

Think about how your growth mindset has developed over the last five years. Write a letter to your growth mindset.

MY DAY AT SCHOOL   Date:

MY DAY AT SCHOOL   Date:

....

....

....

....

....

....

....

....

....

....

....

....

....

....

....

....

....

MY DAY AT SCHOOL   Date:

....

....

....

....

....

....

....

....

....

....

....

....

....

....

....

....

MY DAY AT SCHOOL   Date:

....

....

....

....

....

....

....

....

....

....

....

....

....

....

....

....

MY DAY AT SCHOOL

Date:

MY DAY AT SCHOOL

Date:

MY DAY AT SCHOOL

Date:

MY DAY AT SCHOOL   Date:

....

....

....

....

....

....

....

....

....

....

....

....

....

....

....

....

MY DAY AT SCHOOL   Date:

....

....

....

....

....

....

....

....

....

....

....

....

....

....

....

....

MY DAY AT SCHOOL   Date:

....

....

....

....

....

....

....

....

....

....

....

....

....

....

....

....

MY DAY AT SCHOOL   Date:

....

....

....

....

....

....

....

....

....

....

....

....

....

....

....

....

MY DAY AT SCHOOL   Date:

MY DAY AT SCHOOL   Date:

MY DAY AT SCHOOL   Date:

MY DAY AT SCHOOL   Date:

....

....

....

....

....

....

....

....

....

....

....

....

....

....

....

....

....